FRID. AVGVSTI II
DVCIS SAXON. S.R.I.ELECTORIS
NEC NON REGIS POLONIAE CVRA
PATRI ET ANTECESSORI
POSITVM.
A.D.MDCCXXXVI.

Beautiful
DRESDEN

Klaus-Jürgen Vetter (Editor)

CONTENTS

◄◄ THE GILDED MONUMENT OF AUGUST THE STRONG on Horseback on the Neustädter Market.

◄ DRESDEN, THE PANORAMA – with Frauenkirche, Brühlsche Terrasse and river steamboats

"Dresden is a delightful and, with permission, may I add that it is a place which I would never want to leave."

Johann Wolfgang v. Goethe

VERBUM DOMINI MANET IN AETERNUM. LAUS TIBI DEO SPES MEA IN DEO EST

ERNST. FRIEDRICH D. SANFTMUETHIGE. ALBRECHT D. BEHERZTE. FRIEDRICH D. WEISE. JOHANN D. BESTAENDIGE. JOHANN FRIEDRICH D. G
1464–1486. 1428–1464. 1486–1500. 1486–1525. 1525–1532.

◄ THE CAPITAL OF SAXONY is the political and geographical center of the Land Saxony, one of 17 Länder that compose Germany. Dresden looks back on a history of 800 years, long stretches of which were inextricably bound up with the dynasty of the House of Wettin. The picture at right shows a section of the so-called "Fürstenzug", procession of princes, but to be more precise Guelph margraves, electors, and kings, who ruled Saxony from the time of Konrad the Great (1123–1156) to George, the penultimate king of the line (1902-1904). Such stones of Dresden bear witness in our own day to the stately creativity of these rulers. Much of it survived the city's numerous conflagrations as well as the catastrophe of the Second World War. During the period of the German Democratic Republic (1949–1989) many of Dresden's treasures were maintained or even restored, but much was also unrestorably destroyed. With Germany's reunification rebuilding was given new impetus. "The Florence of the Elbe," Germany's counterpart to Italy's Florence on the Arno River, nowadays radiates forth beauty that is both historically new and historically restored. The star performance in demonstration of this was the restoration and reopening of the mighty Frauenkirche, the city's Protestant cathedral that was destroyed during a Dresden air raid in the Second World War. The Frauenkirche apart, here's scarcely another European city in which one great tourist site so consistently jostles the next, with the lot of them authenticated by the sinuous signature of the broad and placid Elbe River. Be it the "Zwinger," one of the great treasures of the German version of baroque, or the (erstwhile) royal Residenz, or the museums and other cultural sites such as the Semper Opera, Dresden is everything except jejune.

▼ **DRESDEN, THE PANORAMA.** Large tracts of Dresden were destroyed during February 1945, in a rain of wartime bombs dropped by the Allies. The rest of the damage followed after the war when the East German regime, satellite to the Moscow style, started filling the gaps with konstruktion-kit projects. But the serious remedial effort exerted over the past few years has helped a great deal. The famous Dresden panorama, as shown in our picture, stretches from the Frauenkirche to the Roman Catholic Hofkirche, church of the court. Flanked by the two great churches is the "Brühlsche Terrasse", so called because it was ordered up by the Count of Brühl (1700-1763) a government minister in the reign of his master, the Elector Friedrich August II (1696–1763).

▼▼ **BRÜHLSCHER GARTEN.** The "garden", really more like a small park, is named after Count Brühl. Its greenery and flora are backdropped by the Frauenkirche along with a tract of buildings collectively called the Albertinum, which contains three museums.

▶▼ **THE LUTHER MONUMENT.** Fronting the Frauenkirche stands, eminently visible, the monument of Martin Luther. It had to be war-repaired before being put back where history commanded it to display itself.

▶ **FRAUENKIRCHE.** Presenting a picture that nowadays belongs to the past: it shows the Frauenkirche during its long postwar state when scaffolding enfolded it. Rebuilding started in 1993 and some of the funding for it came from abroad. As a gesture of reconciliation, and perhaps of contrition, the Duke of Kent presented the rebuilt church with its new, eight meter-high, finial cross.

◀◀ THE FRAUENKIRCHE, emblem of the city, is once more on show in its old splendor. The story of the church reaches back to the eleventh century when the present edifice's predecessor was Dresden's main Roman Catholic parish church. In a series of updatings, stone started being used as a building material in the thirteenth and fourteenth for a basilica. A conversion and enlargement to a Gothic hall-style followed. Finally, in the first half of the sixteenth century, the church was converted to a late-Gothic. In the immediate wake of the Reformation the building temporarily ceased being a church but later in the century it reopened. The church in its present form is the chef d'oeuvre of the city council's master carpenter George Bähr (1666–1738). Once construction started, it only took three years for building to attain the top rafters. Originally the cupola was to have been constructed of wood but at Bähr's insistence stone was used instead. After his decease, Johann Georg Schmidt, who had been trained by Bähr, finished the project. But he built Bähr's cupola more lightly than had been intended by Schmidt's master.

▲◀ VIEW FROM THE ELBE'S NEW-TOWN SIDE. The cupola of the Frauenkirche dominates the city's skyline. At right in the picture, the neo-renaissance-style guildhall. It is now the seat of Saxony's Superior Court.

▲◀ ART ACADEMY AND FRAUENKIRCHE. The monument in front of the Art Academy is that of Gottfried Semper (1803–1879) and celebrates one of Dresden's great architects. In the background, the Frauenkirche.

◀ DOLPHIN FOUNTAIN AT THE ALBERTINUM. This piece of statuary showing a boy and a dolphin is the only item to survive of the original ensemble of Brühl's own time. All the rest of the Brühlsche Terrasse is of a later date.

◀ THE CUPOLA of the Frauenkirche is a proud 95 meters high. The church itself has a capacity of 3,600. Dresdeners long opposed the rebuilding of the church, wanting the ruins to stand as a memento mori of the Second World War. The raid that destroyed the church also killed between 25,000 and 40,000 human beings. The fire inside the Frauenkirche was so intense that it destroyed all its furnishings including the precious Silbermann organ. Sandstone in the church's structural materials baked itself into fragility and, as a consequence, the entire building collapsed two days after the raid. After the reunification of Germany the time finally arrived for rebuilding. At the initiative of Dresden's citizenry a world-wide fund-raising campaign was started. The federal government and that of Land Saxony chipped in to round out what was needed. Former war enemies also contributed, foremost the British. In all, the reconstruction cost about 170 million euros. In rebuilding the church every stone in the ruin was carefully catalogued, cleaned, newly dressed and then re-used in its original place.

In June, 2003, in time for the Feast of the Pentecost, the bells of the church rang anew. On 30 October 2005, the Frauenkirche was festively reopened with a celebrative service. With that, Dresden had regained its cherished emblem, but one having a new sense, as one of reconciliation.

▼ THE BRÜHLSCHE TERRASSE. The cupola of the Frauenkirche over looms a site that originally, in the eighteenth century, served as a fortification. The site retains very little of that character. Count Brühl caused a garden to be built here. In the succeeding decade he had Master Builder Christof Knöffel (1688-1752), a man celebrated by art history as the founder of the Saxon rococo style, fill out the site with an ensemble of buildings. Alas, none of this work has survived, though replacements heeded the old feel of the place. Today there may be found there the New Guildhall, an edifice known as the Sekundogenitur, and the Art Academy with its collection of noted masters.

▶ **Gingerbread and Cake-Loaf.** At Yuletide the square fronting the Frauenkirche turns into a Christmas market. The smell of Glühwein and grilling sausages fills the air. Stalls occupy the space, selling figurines of the Nativity and its other components; a variety of traditional Christmas decorations notably such Saxon specialities as "Christmas pyramids", Schwibbogen (semicircles of thin wood in which are carved Christmas motifs), carved wooden figurines with jaws that serve as a nutcracker (from Saxony), along with whatever else the Christmassy heart may desire.

▶ **Striezelmarkt.** The Christmas market with any even longer tradition than the Fauenkirche's, indeed Germany's paradigm, is the so-called "Striezelmarkt" that sets up annually in Dresden's Altmarkt Square, old market square. The Striezelmarkt's seniority is attested by a document dating back to 1434. The name derives from that of a baked good that contains raisins steeped in rum, orange extract, lemon extract, and frequently also almonds. This Dresden version of a Christmas pudding began being sold in the sixteenth century. But over the passage of time the baked good originally called Striezel became far better known under the term "Stollen. Today the "Dresdener Christstollen" is exported worldwide in brisk competition with Nuremberg's gingerbread.

▶▶ **Church of the Saxon Court.** The Roman Catholic cathedral of The Holy Trinity, also known as the Court Church, has a floor area of almost five thousand square meters, making it Saxony's largest church. It was erected between 1739 (emplacement of corner stone) and 1755 in the reign of August III, the son of August the Strong. It is a church whose design was designed to convey a political message. How so? Well, August the Strong had renounced his Protestant faith and turned Roman Catholic so that he could be elected King of (Roman Catholic) Poland.

◄ FESTIVAL TOWN. Dresden is a city renowned for its great festivals as well as for its lesser festivities. A bloom of fireworks such as accompanies not every occasion is here shown lending the Frauenkirche a fiery gloriole. Music plays a special role. Dresden has been a stage to music for so long that by now it's become a tradition. Noteworthy in this regard is Music Festival time that stretches from late in May to early in June. The Festival's usual fare includes some one hundred concerts featuring well-known ensembles and soloists from all over. Performances take place at a variety of sites, palaces, churches, and theaters. As of a few years back, the accustomed formality of the festival program loosened up and began to accommodate almost all tastes in music. Aside from classical offerings there are top-quality ones featuring Jazz and other global styles. Since 2003 the festival has become thematic, stressing some specific-stage of music. A further Dresden event is the so-called Elbhang (on the bank of the Elbe), a geographic name for a stretch of Saxony lying on the Elbe and spotted between the communities of Loschwitz and Pillnitz. End of June is festival time there. Along seven kilometers of the Elbe, in parks, village squares, and on the shores of five communities, the festival takes the form of a combined village and regional blow-out. It is very popular with Dresdeners but also draws visitors from other regions.

◄ DIXIELAND FESTIVAL. Annually in May Dresden plays host to the International Dixieland Festival, the largest of its kind in Europe. Numerous bands from all over the world are yearly invited: During festival time the city resounds with the swingin' blare of Dixieland Jazz.

The parade that marches through the city to cap the festival has established itself as an important folk fest.

◄◄ THE ZWINGER. The Dresden Zwinger, picture at far left, is a lofty, perhaps paradigmatic, example of the Baroque style of architecture. It was built between 1711 and 1728 by Matthäus Daniel Pöppelmann (1662-1736) as "a dream in sandstone," as some would have it. It is Pöppelmann's chef d'oeuvre. Statuary art associated with the Zwinger is the work of Balthasar Permoser (1625-1732 and other Dresden sculptors. The term "Zwinger" derives from the name used in medieval fortification for the space between the outer and inner defense perimeters. And Pöppelmann's building happens to be situated in the Zwinger-space between the two old lines of fortification. Originally this space was to have been converted plaza for grandiose festivities such as already existed in Florence, Paris, and Vienna. But the baroque manner of feasting, of indulging in the spectacular, lasted only a bare score of years. Thereafter society came to prefer a more intimate mode. The buildings have since then be used to store and exhibit precious collections of various varieties of art.

◄◄ THE GLOCKENSPIEL PAVILION. The Pavilion shown in our picture, below far left, is part of the complex consisting of an inner court, arcaded halls, and four pavilions. The court measures one hundred-sixteen meters in length and one hundred-seventeen in breadth. Arcaded halls on all sides, except the one facing the Elbe River, surround it. The pavilions mark the four corner of the court. The Glockenspiel pavilion, designed in the eighteenth century, came to justify its name only belatedly when, in 1930, it finally was provided with its glockenspiel.

▲◄ WINTER SCENE. A panoramic view from the Kronentor (left in picture) to the celebrated Wallpavillion (right).

◄ THE WALLPAVILLION. Here it is, as seen through a fountain' spume fronting it. Some opinion rates the Wall pavilion as Pöppelmann's best piece of work.

◄ THE PORCELAIN MUSEUM. Near the Glockenspielpavillion and accessible from the Theaterplatz, theater square, lies a part of the Zwinger that houses one of the greatest collections of porcelain. August the Strong was a passionate collector and sowed the seed of a collection featuring items that have remained famous to this day. On display are examples from Japan, China, and Meissen. Among the most spectacular of the exhibits surely rank the large Meissen figurines created from a material that some call "white gold".

▼ OLD MASTERS. Among the highlights of any visit to Dresden almost surely ranks the time spent with the old masters in the Zwinger's Gemäldegallerie, gallery of paintings. The gallery is splendidly located in the so-called Semperbau, Semper building, named after the talented architect who built it, Gottfried Semper. Some seven hundred-sixty European paintings, dating from the fourteenth to the eighteenth centuries, are displayed here. The collection includes works as famous as Raphael's Sistine Madonna (our picture shows it as seen through a door that is ajar). This particular painting was obtained in 1754, but other acquisitions date back farther and include masterpieces by Dürer, Titian, Rubens, Rembrandt, and Holbein. Today's collection roots in one started by an Electoral Chamber of Art founded in 1560 and then notably enlarged with precious items by August the Strong.

►► THE RESIDENZ (see spread that follows). The royal castle with its arresting sgrafitti façade underwent much alteration over its span of centuries. Originally a medieval fortified castle occupied the site (thirteenth century) and only in the sixteenth was it gussied into a monarch's abode. There was a disastrous fire in 1701 and from there the castle's history of alterations limped forward until the nineteenth century when it was given the style that it has since worn, neo-Renaissance. Destroyed in World War II – except for part of its precious "Grünes Gewölbe" (green arcade) – it was eventually rebuilt and opened again in 2006.

▼ **GRÜNES GEWÖLBE – CABINET OF AMBER.** The Residenz today houses the State Art Collections. In one part of the "Grünes Gewölbe" (Green Arcade) is to be found the so-called amber cabinet, a present to the Saxon royal house from Prussia's King Wilhelm I. On display there is what has become a very famous collection of artifice in amber. Our picture shows one of the displays, legended as "The Great Basin" (1605).

▼▼ **CHAMBER OF JEWELRY.** The Green Arcade gets its name from the malachite marble that partly covers the walls of the ground floor in west wing,

walls that elsewhere are simply painted green.

▼ **HALL OF PRECIOUSNESS.** The so-called Pretiosensaal (picture, upper right) has an impressive-enough floor area of two hundred-twelve square meters, yet looks much bigger. That is because its walls are generously endowed with mirrors to reflect the room's sweep as well as its carved ornamentation. On display, among other items, are bowls of precious stone and vessels of mountain crystal.

▼▼ **CHAMBER OF BRONZE.** The walls here are paneled in oak. They vouch-

safe an appropriate air to the display of some eighty bronzes, partly mounted on pedestals or consoles. Our picture, at bottom right, shows August the Strong, mounted a-horse, rendered in a bronze statue, mounted on a pedestal.

▶ **HAUSMANNSTURM.** The oldest remainder of the original castle is thought to be the square base of the Hausmannsturm (guard tower) in the old castle's west wing. The Hausmannsturm is thought to have been built to guard the bridges and ferry traffic across the Elbe.

◄◄ GRÜNES GEWÖLBE – CHAMBER OF JEWELRY. Walls here are gilded; mirroring and back-of-glass painting find generous use. Primarily featured are ensembles of jewelry, though some are are not complete.

◄ IVORY CHAMBER. Encompassed here is the oldest part of the Gewölbe's collection. Walls are paneled in marble; carved and lathe-worked items, such as candelabra and filigree figurines, abound, They may have been on display for almost measureless stretches of time but the ivory still does what it is supposed to do: it gleams.

◄ THE WHITE SILVER CHAMBER'S GRANDFATHER CLOCK. The ninety-five square meters of this chamber are enclosed by walls strikingly painted in vermilion. In conjunction with the chamber's mirroring it lends a warmly stately setting for the objects here displayed. August the Strong loved everything mechanical and collected clocks. These star here, and notably among them is our grandfather clock.

The chambers of the Historical Green Arcade remained closed after the Second World War but reopened to the public in 2006. The collection contains more than three thousand displayed items. But as none are protected in vitrines the number of visitors flowing past anti-dust sluices at the entrance is limited to a rate of one hundred in an hour. That means that only eight hundred visitor may pass in any one day when the collection is open. Reservations are therefore required and these are obtainable via the Internet.

▶ **IVORY STATUARY IN THE WHITE SILVER CHAMBER.** Shown here in ivory is the climax of the Old Testament's story of Abraham. It is the moment when the angel stays the hand of the Father of the Jews as he, following the command of the Lord, is about to slay his beloved son Isaac. A memorial in ivory to Abraham's faith and trust in God.

▶▶ **THE "EMERALD MOOR".** A wood sculpture executed by Balthasar Permoser and splendidly bejeweled by the atelier of Johann Melchior Dinglinger (Dresden, 1724). Proffered on the Moor's tray is what ostensibly is a matrix of emeralds. Originally touted as a mineralogical rarity from Colombia it is today known to be an imitation – which does not necessarily diminish its value, considering its significance to a genuinely precious ensemble. The emerald was a present to the Saxon Elector August (1526–1568) from his friend King Rudolf II on the occasion of a visit by August to Rudolf's capital, Prague. The sculpture of the moor is of a much later date and was only then integrated with the "emerald". The figure, sculpted of pear wood, is some sixty-three centimeters high, finished in tortoise-shell veneer, varnished dark brown. Emeralds, rubies, sapphires, topazes, and garnets make of the moor and his tray a veritable bearer of all that is precious. As it turns out, the term "moor" is also faux. The sculptured likeness is not of a black African, but of an American native.

◄ CIGAR MANUFACTORY "YENIDZE". The extraordinary building shown here, an exotic example of modern industrial architecture, was built in the years 1907–1909. Its unusual name somehow hints at its initial purpose. The hint is apposite because the name derives from that of a small tobacco-growing area of Greece which, at the time of the building's erection still, belonged to the Ottoman Empire. Hence the tobacco factory's resemblance to a mosque, a veritable Ottoman symbol. The history of the building is about as odd as are its looks. The industrialist Hugo Zietz specified the style in order to circumvent the building code. The code forbade erection in the city's core of any building with smoke stacks. But it did not forbid minarets, so it's there that Hugo Zietz concealed the factory's single smoke stack, inside one of the minarets. The architect Adolph Hammitzsch was selected to fashion this industrial blind. In his design he followed the oriental model, in main the tombs of the caliphs in Cairo. The great dome is especially rich in ornamentation. Its generous use of colored glass appears to seek to overwhelm the visitor. But kismet being kismet, the building ceased being a factory long ago. Nowadays it houses cultural events such as literary readings and belly-dance soirees.

◄ MUSEUM OF SAXON FOLK ART, located in the so-called Jägerhof (hunter's court) offers a display of folk art from all of Saxony's regions. Exhibits take the form of painted rural furniture (picture below), needlework, Christmas crèches and associated Nativity figures, step pyramids, old toys, and other products of Saxony's artisan tradition.

To be seen also, at left, are the renderings of two beehives as wooden statues (man and woman) dating back to the middle of the eighteenth century. The museum may be recommended for children (who usually have little patience with Great Art) especially as a collection of dolls was added around 2005.

Dresden is known for its collection of Old Masters, but there's another gallery, that dedicated to the work of the New Masters and which experts deem worthy of a visit. Among its exhibits are capital works by such painters of the romantic school as Caspar David Friedrich, Ludwig Richter, and of the painter who was also a physician and naturalist, Carl Gustav Carus. A wide range of works by German impressionists is also part of the museum's collection and contains works by such artists as Max Liebermann, Lovis Corinth, and Max Slevogt. There is also a sculpture collection, which ranges from the times of antiquity to those of the recent past. The accent here is on works of antiquity.

Those interested in literature and music will be made to feel at home in Dresden. Born in 1899 in Dresden was Erich Kaestner, the author of, among other more ponderous works, "Emil and the Detectives." Votive to him is a museum located in the space of the Villa Augustin, which once belonged to his uncle. The author not only of "Emil" but also of other best-selling books for adult readers gets a multimedial showing in his museum.

The Carl-Maria-von-Weber museum commemorates the Kapellmeister of the Dresden Opera (from 1817 to 1826, the year of his passing) and his most famous work, the romantic opera "Freischütz," a key work in Germany's span of art.

◀◀ **THE FÜRSTENZUG.** One of Dresden's most remarkable sights is this "procession of princes", which is to say the likenesses of almost all of historic monarchs of Saxony's dynastic House of Wettin. It takes the form of a frieze, more than one hundred meters in length and nine hundred-fifty square meters in area. It was commissioned to mark the eight hundredth anniversary of the enfeoffment by Emperor Heinrich IV of the Margrave Heinrich von Eilenburg with the March of Meissen. In the procession of monarchs he is the first, while was Georg (1902–1904) brings up the rear. At the very tail end of the procession are to be seen the painters and other artisans involved in the production of the frieze. It was completed in the summer of 1907 but was based on a design dating back to 1867.

◀◀ **PFUND'S DAIRY.** At first visit to Dresden one should not fail to take it in. It is the town's oldest and most traditional shoppe dealing in milk and cheese. Yes, Pfund's Dairy is the plain name of the place. For Dresdners it is the most beautiful cheese boutique in the world. Walls and ceilings are inlaid with tiles in the fashion of the Jugendstil, belle époque, hand painted to show scenes associated with the boutique's offerings, milch cows, or depictions of dairy procedures such as the manufacture of cheese and the milking of cows. Paul Gustav Pfund (1849–1923) opened his store in 1892. Back then there was a window through which customers could view the milking of the dairy's bovines. They could even specify the cow whose milk they wanted to buy. Between the choice of cow and payment for purchase, the milk would be filtered and cooled.

◀ **PROCESSION OF STEAMERS.** The Elbe's traditional paddle-wheeled steamers still figure in today's Dresden as a popular way to rubberneck the river.

◀ **ELBE NOCTURNE,** featuring the illuminated Hofkirche (left), Semper's opera house (right), plus excursion shipping.

◀ SHOPPING. Dresden's character is by no mean entirely artistic and cultural. For centuries the town that grew into a city also figured as a business center. And so it came to pass that in our day it built itself a so-called World Trade Center, a sprawling office building-cum shopping mall. Built in the years 1993-1997 ambitioned to stand for the upward mobile and newly prospering Dresden. Its address is on the Freibergerstrasse. Geographic location and historical networking could be said to have predestined the town for a key role in trade between the East and the West. If so, then Dresden's World Trade Center copuld have been built to redeem that prospect. The Center consists of seven buildings and a glass tower fifty-three meters in height. The Center's mall has an arched ceiling of glass and steel. Facades are partly dressed in sandstone. The complex has its own theater, restaurants, and cafes.

▼ THE OLD MARKET'S NEW SHOPPING CENTER. The Galerie am Altmarkt, gallery on the old market, has a commercial surface of 25,000 square meters encompassing four floors. It holds a hundred stores, restaurants, and cafes and caters to a variety of taste and purse. Entrance is via the Old Market or the pedestrian mall on the Prager Strasse. Itplays host, daily, to some 30,000 shoppers and browsers.Shops specialized in international fashion and its accessories are located on the other shore of the Elbe in what is called the New Town. in the area between the Hauptstrasse and the Königstrasse. Handicraft is bunched in passage-like malls fronting on the Hauptstrasse.

Of relevance is also the so-called Kunsthofpassage, art court mall, in the Äussere Dresdener Neustadt, outer new town of Dresden, between the addresses of Alaunstrasse 70 and Görlitzer Strasse 21-75. Here is located a complex of courts in which each court has shops votive to some theme: wares having to do with fable, lighting, animals, etc. Among the et ceteras are pubs, multimedia arcades, as well as a variety of exhibitions. Miscellany on sale.

▶ **THE TASCHENBERG PALACE.** It stands on a height of the Elbe's bank and is the first great work of the architectissimo Matthäus Daniel Pöppelmann. He built the palace on commission from August the Strong for his mistress Anna Constantia von Brockdorff, later assuming the guise of the Imperial Countess Cosel, and the station of the premier lady of the Elector's court. The palace took five years to build, 1707 to 1712. But revisions followed and the palace in its final form only materialized in 1763. Largely destroyed during World War II, the palace has in the meantime been entirely restored. Today it is home to a hotel, the Kempinski Hotel Taschenbergpalais – one of the leading hostelries of Dresden.

▶ **HOTEL DE SAXE.** Once a town palace – or "hotel" in the old French sense of the word – and bearing the name of its aristocratic owner, it is now a hotel in the modern sense, the Steigenberger Hotel de Saxe. The façade of the new hotel is a remake of the original "hotel's" until 1888. Now as then it stands on the Neumarkt, new market, in the center of the Altstadt, old town. A mark of interest is the so-called Luther Stone, now to be seen to the right of the hotel's entrance. It is a replica of a stone to be found near the church of St. Aphra in Meissen. Graven on the stone are the first four capital letters of the alphabet so intertwined that, with some effort, one can make out all the letters of the alphabet. The stone was said to have been intended to commemorate Luther's translation into German of the bible.

▶▶ **WINTER MOOD** ... a square snowed in, a Hausmannsturm illuminated, a city mantled in silense....

▶▶ **SEMPEROPER** (picture spread that follows). Dresden's opera house is known by the name of its builder, (Gottfried) Semper, the architect who put his stamp on Dresden's style in the nineteenth century – as had Pöppelmann in the eighteenth.

◄◄ THE NEW OPERA. The Semper Opera's current official label is "Saxon State Opera, Dresden." This does not alter the fact that the house remains better known by the name of its architect, (Gottfried) Semper. Actually today's opera house is the third to follow Semper's original one. The first house, built between 1838 and 1841, burned down in 1869. The second try, designed by Semper himself and only after his death completed by his eldest son Manfred, took from 1871 and 1878. The third house was a little different in that it was erected at a new site. Opera No.2 was larger than its predecessor and more modern in design, especially in the specifications for its stage and associated apparatus. It was Opera No.3 that was destroyed in the air raid of February 1945. Reconstruction began in the 70's and was completed in 1985.

▲◄ EQUESTRIAN MONUMENT. This shows King Johann of Saxony (1801-1873) who caused the opera to be built. The statue was fashioned in bronze by Johannes Schilling (1801-1873). Johann's reign spanned the years 1854-1873. His signal attribute, rare among monarchs, was scholarship.

◄◄ PANTHERQUADRIGA. Surmounting the opera's massive and ornate portal is Johann Schilling's – the same of the equestrian statue – tour de force showing four panthers drawing a chariot with Dionysus, father of wine, and Ariadne, mother of barley, as its passengers. At ground level the opera's entrance is ornamented with sculptures of Goethe and Schiller; niches lateral to the portal house statues of a selection of the world's great dramatists.

◄ BAROQUE COSTUMES. Our picture shows some actors appropriately garbed to reinforce for our day the idea of the historical relation of the opera to the role Dresden claims for itself as a cultural venue.

I. RANG

◀ **Opera Vestibule.** The Semper Opera pretends the style of the neo-Renaissance. It is eighty-four meters wide and some seventy-seven meters high; it has five floors. On the fortieth anniversary of its destruction the house revived with a performance of Carl Maria von Weber's "Freischütz." The choice of 13 February 1985 as the reopening date was as poignant as the choice of "Freischütz." Together they were meant as a reminder that precisely this opera had been the last to be performed before the house's wartime destruction. Later on, the architect Wolfgang Hänsch, who happens to have been born in the vicinity of Dresden, supervised reconstruction. The vestibule, with its magnifi-cent ceiling painting, as shown in our picture, is one of the opera's most ornate spaces.

▼ **Auditorium and Stage.** The opera is renowned for its acoustics. It accommodates 1,300, which has helped to make it one of the most fre-quented opera houses in all of Europe. As the home of the Saxon State Band, Dresden, Sächsische Staatskapelle Dresden, it automatically something that calls itself a mere "band" with the cachet of a major-league German orchestra – and one having an espe-cially long tradition, at that. Its forma-tion dates back to the sixteenth centu-ry and the reign of the Elector Moritz of Saxony. Among its chief founding conductors were Carl Maria von Weber and Richard Wagner. A partial list of more recent ones includes Fritz Reiner, Fritz Busch, Karl Böhm, Joseph Kelbert, Kurt Sanderling, and Guiseppe Sinopoli. The Semper Opera has served as the cradle for numerous world premieres, e.g. Wagner's "Rien-zi" (1842), "The Flying Dutchman" (1843), and "Tannhäuser" (1845) – all these in House No.1 – and then, in House No. 2, highlights of Richard Strauss' period, namely "Salome" (1905), based on a work by Oscar Wilde, and most notably two operas that Strauss did in collaboration with the poet Hugo von Hofmannsthal, "Elektra" (1909) and "Rosenkavalier" (1910) – the latter certainly still the most popular of Strauss' operas.

◄ **THE GREAT GARDEN AND PALACE.** The Grosse Garten, great garden, is Dresden's oldest and largest park. Located to the southwest of the Old Town it orients rather more to the periphery and the city's main railroad station. Almost 35 kilometers of paths have helped to make the park a favorite excursion site with the locals, but also an attraction for tourists and other visitors. Anyone overcome by fatigue during a ramble can seek remedy by retreating to the park's own railroad that provides circumferential transport. The park offers a number of leisure pursuits. For instance one can rent boats and row them on the park's Carola See, lake Carola, named after Queen Carola of Wasa (1833–1907). There is also a park theater that offers both movies and concerts.

Documentation cites 1676 as the year in which the initial purchase of land for the park took place – land that back in that day was farther removed from the inner city limits than it is today. Construction of the palace was begun in 1678 by Johann Georg Starcke and was completed in 1683. The palace is understood to represent Dresden's first piece of baroque architecture. It was built as a residence for a Wettin who was to become Elector of Saxony, Georg III (1647–1691). The style may be baroque but tends to look like a mixture of a relaxed Italian pleasure palace and a formal French one.

The park itself was laid out following the era's French taste. The architect in charge was Johann Friedrich Karcher (1650–1726). Typical of its French genre are the straight lanes and the central location within the park of the palace itself. Also the great reflecting pool. Only a little of the park's original statuary still remains on view, but among the survivors is the remarkable marble ensemble called "Time Abducts Beauty" (foreground, in our picture). The sculptor is Pietro Balestra, first half of the seventeenth century.

◄◄ FUNICULAR. A Dresden curio is the funicular railway that connects a part of town called Weisser Hirsch, white stag, with down-to-earth Dresden, one hundred meters below it, and five hundred forty-seven meters distant. The contrivance has been operating since 1895. This may explain why the Stadtseilbahn Loschwitz, Loschwitz municipal funicular, is popularly thought of as one of Dresden's most significant technical monuments. A ticket on the funicular will buy you a precious view of the city.

◄ OLDE DEPOT. This is where the Loschwitz funicular's journey starts, the journey to the view and the inn. Four minutes is what the trip takes. The average speed is 20 kilometers per hour. Midway, the funicular rattles over a bridge that is some one hundred meters long and twelve meters above the ground. Near both of the terminals the funicular passes through tunnels. Until 1905 it was steam-driven and originally not intended for passenger traffic. Rather, it transported building materials in special cars. Only after electrification did the funicular begin catering to human adventurers.

◄ VIEW FROM THE "BERGSCHWEBEBAHN". Not far from the funicular there is another cable contrivance that is a part of local tradition, the Bergschwebebahn, aerial tram. Launched in 1901 by the Crown Prince Friedrich August, later King August III, it negotiates a steep stretch measuring 274 meters in length and 80 at maximum altitude from the ground below.

◄ WINTER IN THE PARK. In Loschwitz the recommended thing to do is a visit of Eckberg Castle and its park. The castle was built between 1859 and 1861 in the neo-Gothic style. And it survived World War II almost unscathed.

►► BLUE WONDER (spread of pages that follow) is what the locals, in a spirit of arch endearment, call their their olde Loschwitzer Brücke, Loschwitz bridge (over the Elbe), nee 1893.

◄ RADEBERG AND DRESDEN'S ENVIRONS.
Tradition also plays a major role in the
areas surrounding the Saxon capital. Radeberg, situated northeast of Dresden on the
edge of the Dresden heath lands, is only
one example among many. The little town
is known nationwide for its Pilsner beer,
which is marketed all over Germany and
was an export hit even during GDR times
(yet was almost unavailable for GDR citizens). The town is also home to a so-
called "Spielmannszug" (in the picture), a
marching band with drums, timbales and
wind instruments that mostly performs
folk- and march music. Today, the group is
comprised of members from the Radeberg
sports club. The band was formed in 1968
and performs in historical Saxon uniforms
at shooting matches or carnival proces-
sions, ever creating sensation and good
humor.

However, the surrounding areas of
Dresden offer much more. They definitely
are rich in history: Throughout the area
traces of the Wettins can be found, albeit
the different cities also developed their
own, distinctive characters respectively.
Whether in the porcelain town of Meissen
or in Radebeul in the middle of the Saxon
wine region, the smallest and northern-
most in Germany, with its centuries old
tradition; whether in Pirna, Pillnitz, Wehlen
or Rathen – Dresden's environs are so rich
in art and natural treasures that they sur-
pass anyone's expectations. One has to go
and experience it for oneself. This is best
done walking or cycling on the most popular bicycle path in Germany, the "Elberad-
weg". For those who like it more comfort-
able, the traditional paddle steamers offer
cruises on the Elbe river.

▼ **MEISSEN.** We start west of Dresden in Meissen. The wine and porcelain town looks back on 1000 years of history; already back in 928 Heinrich I. erected a castle for the protection of the Elbe river line here. The name might stem from "Misni", today's creek Meisa – that is at least how Thietmar von Merseburg (975-1018), historian and bishop of Merseburg, interpreted it. The Late Gothic town hall (in the picture below) certainly is one of the most impressive buildings of its kind. It was built around 1472 and has been remodeled several times since.

▼▼ **PORCELAIN – THE WHITE GOLD.** The history of European porcelain begins with the apothecary assistant Johann Friedrich Böttger (1682-1719), whom August the Strong (August der Starke) took into his service as a gold wright. Böttger was an alchemist, and the alchemy of the time had as its main goal the production of gold. These days we know that this could not have worked. Nevertheless, these experiments produced a number of discoveries, even though their interpretation today raises a smile. One of the most momentous findings surely

was that Böttger in 1709 found out how to produce white porcelain. August the Strong promptly recognized the potential of the "white gold". Thus, since 1710, there has been the world-renowned Meissen porcelain with the signet of the two crossed swords. The precious pieces are still hand painted (see pictures).

▼▶ **ALBRECHTSBURG CASTLE AND CATHEDRAL.** Two of the most impressive buildings of Meissen are the Early Gothic sandstone cathedral (building start around 1266), and Albrechtsburg Castle (end of 17th century).

◀ **GATE HOUSE IN MEISSEN.** The central castle gate of Albrechtsburg Castle Meissen today houses part of the Meissen town museum. The gate once protected the access to the castle; now furniture and paintings from the Biedermeier time (first half of 19th century) can be viewed here.

▼ **ALBRECHTSBURG CASTLE IN MEISSEN.** The silver mines in the Ore Mountains made it possible: the glorious castle was funded through returns from the mining and sale of the precious metal, which flourished in the 15th century. Thus a magnificent building emerged, which for a short period, in place of the old margrave castle, served as residence to the Wettins (however soon after its completion the princes moved to Dresden). Construction was begun in 1471 under Arnold von Westfalen and basically completed around 1485. Damaged badly during the Thirty Years' War, the building was restored in the second half of the 17th century. Between 1710 and 1864, the castle accommodated the Meissen Porcelain Manufactory.

The building is an important witness to the changes in German castle architecture. It marks the transition from the medieval castle to the palace. For the first time, all the rooms of one floor had the same elevation and, unlike the old castles, came with very large windows. In some aspects, the influence of French palatial architecture can be seen: so in the skylight windows or the so-called gable lucarnes, which were very popular in the 16th century. These roof superstructures in the form of a multi-story house appear at a right angle with the gable, flushing with the façade. Often copied in German castle architecture was also the stairs tower, set off in front of the façade, which adds to the impression of the façade.

▶▶ **MORITZBURG CASTLE.** The hunting lodge was built between 1542 and 1546 by Elector Moritz of Saxony (1521–1553). In the beginning of the 18th century, extensive remodeling works were carried out, in which Matthäus Daniel Pöppelmann was involved, among others; interior design done by Raymond Leplat.

►► MORITZBURG – "MONSTRÖSENSAAL". This enormous two-story hall dramatically illustrates the display of splendor in Early Baroque. The term "monströs" relates to the numerous antlers hanging on the walls there. Those chosen here were preferably crooked, "monstrous" specimens. Parts of the hunting castle today are accessible as a museum.

► SEATED ON THE WATER. Quite distinctive are the four mighty towers of Moritzburg Castle. Originally built in Renaissance style, later on it no longer seemed to please August the Strong. He therefore had it extensively remodeled and expanded. Pöpelmann got the assignment to transform the castle into a Baroque palace. He enlarged the central part of the castle both in height and width. Four splendor halls were established and bedecked with painted leather wallpaper. A curiosity on the ground floor is the room with feather wallpaper, which is comprised of millions of feathers of Southern American birds. Showing in the picture: the statue of one of the two piqueurs guarding the main approach. The piqueur at a battue is a hunter who seeks out the game and sets the dogs on it. In his hand he is holding a so-called Parforcehorn, a forerunner of the French horn.

► "FASANENSCHLÖSSCHEN". Close by the pheasant park established in 1728, Friedrich August III. commissioned the building of "Fasanenschlösschen" (Pheasant Castle, 1769–1782). The little castle forms a stark contrast in style to Moritzburg Castle in the vicinity. While the latter represents the abundant, rich Early Baroque, still unaffected by the emerging French taste; with Pheasant Castle the line of Rococo is already crossed. Signs of this are the conscious simplicity and the use of forms derived from Antiquity. "Naturalness" was the motto of the time.

▶ **Light House for Ships ?.** While one would usually expect beacons at the sea, the pond of Fasanenschlösschen also features such a tower (around 1780), one of the few interior exemplars. It is part of a miniature harbor facility and never served as an orientation guide for navigation (on this little pond?). Rather it acted, together with the harbor, as an ideal backdrop for amusements. So it was possible, for instance, to effectively include the landscape environment in the display of entire naval battles, a popular form of entertainment in the 18th century. There is also a historic background, however: the Battle at the Dardanelles in the year 1770, where the Russian fleet of Tsarina Catherine the Great defeated the Turkish armada. This triumph over the Ottoman "arch-enemies" was celebrated in the whole of Europe. After this war had ended, the high-ranking Russian officer Count Orlow (1734–1783), a favorite and, at times, a lover of Catherine, visited the Saxon court. Orlow had a leading role in the planning of the battle and the victory against the Ottomans. One year later, the Electress Amalie Auguste reports of the first ride on the Moritzburg pond with a two-masted frigate that had been specifically built for that purpose. Count Camillo Marcolini (1739–1814), who made it from page (Silberpage) at court to the head of the Meißen Porcelain Manufactory, acted as the admiral. A model of the Dardanelles was equipped with canons one could even shoot with – albeit not with real, but only with fireworks munitions.

◄◄ **Radebeul – Wackerbarth Castle**
(Picture left and above). Surrounded by
vineyards this Baroque castle today is the
seat of the Saxon State Wine Estate, which
was founded in 1925. The castle was built
in the years between 1727 and 1730 according to the plans of state master-builder
Johann Christoph Knöffel. It was the retire-
ment place for Count Christoph August
Wackerbarth (1662–1734), who served as
secretary and field marshal under August
the Strong. Especially impressive is the
Belvedere, which is connected to the
palace by an outside staircase. Until 1957
only wine was pressed here, from 1958
also sparkling wine. The sparkling wines
time and again receive international
awards. On the "awc Vienna – international wine challenge", the second largest wine
valuation worldwide, the sparkling wine
"August der Starke" from Wackerbarth
Castle was awarded a gold medal in the
category "Champagne, sparkling wine, car-
bonated wine" in 2006. Today, the castle
calls itself "Europe's first wine estate experience" and offers many tastings and wine
seminars. After all, Germany's northern-
most wine-growing area can look back on
an 800 year tradition.

◄ **Hoflössnitz Castle.** The castle (in
the picture left) built around 1650 under
Elector Johann Georg I. is also surrounded
by vineyards. The simple two-story building today houses the "Museum of Wine-
growing and Culture of Life".

◄ **Karl-May-Museum.** The author Karl
May (1842–1912), inventor of Winnetou
and Old Shatterhand, of Kara Ben Nemsi
and Hadschi Halef Omar – with his adven-
ture novels that are mostly set in America
and the Orient and are widely read until
today, lived in Radebeul from 1895 until his
death. He named his house "Old Shatterhand", where today a museum is dedicated to him.

◄◄ CASTLE GROUNDS PILLNITZ (previous double page). The facility with its spacious park is one of the most beautiful grounds of its kind. Every season the park presents itself from a different but ever attractive side, so that a walk is always worthwhile. The castle used to be the summer residence of the Saxon royal family. Its construction was started under August the Strong, the first part being the "Wasserpalais" (waterside palace; 1720–21). On the side facing away from the Elbe river, in 1723 the "Bergpalais" (hillside palace; in the picture) was built, as almost a laterally reversed image of the "Wasserpalais".

◄ WEESENSTEIN CASTLE. In Pirma district, situated above the Müglitz river, another castle with a long tradition is to be found: Weesenstein Castle, which is considered one of the most beautiful castles of Saxony. The first mention of the grounds occurred in the beginning of the 14th century. The building's most distinctive attribute is its circular tower, which rises higher than anything else. It is at the same time the oldest part (around 1300) of the castle; the bonnet stems from the 18th century. From the 15th until the waning 18th century, it was owned by the counts of Bünau, one of the most influential noble families of Saxony. The house of Bünau branched out widely and was widespread in Bohemia, however researchers do not have an easy time with this family. That is because, according to a family rule, the male descendants of the Bünaus could only have the names Günther, Heinrich and Rudolph. Therefore mix-ups were inevitable. In 1772 the castle came into possession of the Wettins. It was the favored residence of Johann, King of Saxony (1854–1873), whom the rider statue in front of the Semper Opera House in Dresden commemorates. Here he met with scholars and crowned heads from all over Europe.

▼ RIVER STEAMBOAT NEAR PIRNA. The typical excursion boats on the Elbe are paddle-steamers, which are a piece of nostalgia, but are still in use today. Nine of the ships, which are between 78 and 128 years old, operate on steam power today as they did in the past.

▶▶ **PIRNA – CHURCH ST. MARY.** District town Pirna, "the gate to Saxon Switzerland," is an ideal starting point for excursions into the Elbe Sandstone Mountains. But also the town itself has quite something on offer. The great three-nave city church, built in Late Gothic style in the first half of the 16th century and extensively restored in the 19th century, is definitely worth a visit. Upon entering the church, the very wide and spacious room dimensions are immediately striking. Many details catch the eye: among others, a baptismal font with 26 small child figures from 1561, which even Goethe ardently mentioned. By the way, the city name "Pirna" has little to do with "Birne" (pear), even though the city crest shows a pear tree. Today, it is rather assumed that it is derived from the Slavic "na perna", "built on sand stone".

▼ **PIRNA – CHRISTMAS MARKET.** Just like any self-respecting city in Saxony, Pirna, too, has a Christmas market. There is no lack of Saxon specialties here; the scent of Räuchermännchen (traditional incense burners in the shape of little manikins) and mulled wine is all around the city. In the picture below, the market square with the town hall (around 1485, with Late Gothic pointed arch windows and Renaissance gable) and the later-built town hall tower in the center (1718; removed around 1910, then rebuilt to its original state). To its right, Church St. Mary with its mighty tower can be seen. The enormous roof with an overall height of 19.5 meters even surpasses the height of the wall (18 meters).

▶▶ **WEHLEN.** The little town lies only about 25 kilometers upstream along the Elbe at the entrance to the Saxon Switzerland National Park. Whoever plans to stay here and travels by car should enquire beforehand on which side of the Elbe river his accommodation is situated: there is no bridge in Wehlen, only a ferry.

▼ **WEHLEN WITH VILLAGE CHURCH.** This picture nicely illustrates that here the church forms the town center. The place of worship is accordingly old: of an earlier Late Romanesque building the semi-circle apse is still preserved. Especially elaborate and distinctive is the tall west tower (1744). Next to it on the right is a view of the village from the other side of the Elbe river.

▼ **HOHENSTEIN CASTLE** (pictures below and below right, night time view). The picturesque castle on the 140 meter sandstone rock was remodeled and changed time and again. Only in the 17th century, the old wooden buildings were replaced by stone ones, and only in 1806 did the castle irrevocably become part of Saxony. Between 1866 and 1924 it served as a workhouse and jail, from 1925 as a youth hostel. Disreputable was its role during the Nazi regime: in 1933 the Nazis here established one of the first concentration camps. Altogether 5,600 political prisoners were interned here. Since 1948, the castle has been used as a youth hostel once more. A museum is dedicated to the victims of the concentration camp.

▶ **KÖNIGSTEIN FORTRESS.** On a steep mesa, typical for the Elbe Sandstone Mountains, this impressive fortress was erected. Its origins probably reach back to the 12th century, the first reliable mention was in 1241. In the 16th century it was comprehensively extended into a country fortress. Between 1591 and 1922 the fortress was a state prison, which at times held such distinguished prisoners as the Russian anarchist Michael Bakunin (1849) and the Social Democrat August Bebel (1874). Today a museum of military history is set up here.

◄ **FELSENBÜHNE RATHEN.** This natural stage in the middle of the rock scenery of Saxon Switzerland, right beneath the Bastei (bastion) rock formation (from here a stairway of almost 500 steps leads up to Bastei rock), saw the first plays performed here as early as 1936. The open-air-theater since its expansion in the late 50s has 2000 seats. Between June and September, plays and musical shows fitting the scenery are given here, like "Freischütz" and "Hänsel and Gretel". Already in 1938 the first Karl-May-Pageants were held here.

◄◄ **HEALTH RESORT TOWN OF RATHEN** (top left side). Already right in the area of Saxon Switzerland lies this climatic health resort directly at the foot of the mighty rock massif "Bastei". With only 500 citizens, it is one of the smallest townships in Germany. Moreover, the two districts Oberrathen and Niederrathen, the latter on the Bastei-side, are even separated by the Elbe river and can only be reached by a ferry. Rathen is the starting point for many hiking paths leading into the picturesque rock landscape of Saxon Switzerland. Niederrathen, by the way, is car-free. Oberrathen is connected with Dresden via a commuter railway.

◄ **BASTEI BRIDGE.** The bridge consists of 7 arches, is some 76 meters long, 3 meters wide and stretches over a 40 meter deep gorge, the so-called "Mardertelle." It was built in the year 1851.

◄◄ **VIEW OF RATHEN FROM BASTEI ROCK** (bottom left side). This view of the Elbe valley and the small health resort town divided by the river is legendary. No wonder the lookout point attracts so many visitors – a reason why one should get on one's way early.

◄ **ELBE RIVER VIEW.** The Schrammstein rocks, a long stretching, jagged rock group east of Bad Schandau, offer a good view of the Elbe valley.

►► **ELBE RIVER NEAR BAD SCHANDAU.** The sunset creates an enchanting view of the Elbe valley, wraps it in warm colors. Long ago the trees lost their leaves, standing there with their skeleton branches. One could almost believe to be in distant Asia. But it is Germany, it is the Elbe river and we are watching a landscape that is preparing for the cold season.

► **STOLPEN – POST DISTANCE COLUMN.** About 25 km east of Dresden lies the small town of Stolpen with its homonymous castle ruin as a tourist attraction. Of traffic-historical interest is the post league column shown in the picture. During the time of August the Strong, such distance columns were erected at numerous important post and trade routes. This one here in Stolpen is a particularly pretty exemplar. The obelisk-shaped column is lettered on all four sides with indications of the distances to important destinations. All the declarations are in hours, and one can easily imagine how arduous many a trip was in the past. The 25 km to Dresden then required 6 hours, to Meißen it took 11 hours, not to talk about Leipzig, which could only be reached after 30 painful hours. Today even bicycles are faster, let alone the modern means of transportation. Whether the higher speed is really an improvement in this beautiful environment remains undecided …

► **ELBE RIVER CRUISE.** We cannot see what the marveling passengers of this Elbe steamer get to look at, but they are just passing Bastei rock. A good reason to get up from the seats in order to better be able to watch and photograph the grand rock massif.

▼ LANDSCAPE NEAR LOHSDORF (upper two pictures). The little town Lohsdorf in Saxon Switzerland today is a part of Hohnstein. These pictures show that Saxon Switzerland does not just consist of rocks, but has other attractive types of landscape.

The left picture shows a lonely, old chestnut tree in the middle of a meadow. Who would not like to sit in its shade during the summer heat, having a picnic with friends? Next to it, a picture that could also have been taken further to Mecklenburg's north: rapeseed fields abloom in yellow stretching far into the plains. The oil extracted from this rapeseed is processed in edible oils, margarines, shortenings, canned fish and instant meals. In ingredients lists rapeseed oil, like other oils may be classified as "vegetable oil." Rapeseed is also cultivated for the production of animal feed. However, perhaps these fields will also grow our future biodiesel fuel?

▼▼ EXCURSION BOAT WITH BASTEI ROCK IN THE BACKGROUND. The contrast could not be much stronger. Here the flat, wide plains and almost seamlessly next to it, the jagged rock formations of the Bastei and the Elbe Sandstone Mountains.

▼▼ SUNSET. A view of two popular rock climbing cliffs, the "Große Zschand" and, separated from it by the "Roßsteig", the "Kleine Zschand". Many paths in this area are, however, closed for nature conservation reasons.

▶ THE SAXON SWITZERLAND NATIONAL PARK. In 1990, this part of the Elbe Sandstone Mountains about 30 km southeast of Dresden was declared a national park.

◀◀ "TEUFELSSCHLUCHT" (devil's gorge) near Wehlen. If you come from Wehlen following the signposts pointing to "Uttewalder Grund", you can make a trip into the "Teufelsschlucht", a gorge so wild and romantic it lives up to its name. Many a hiker shudders slightly when walking through this wilderness.

◀ VIEW FROM KIPPHORN MOUNTAIN AT SUNSET. About 10 km east of the center of Bad Schandau lies the district Schmilka, very close to the Czech border. Starting there one can venture on a beautiful hike on Winterberg mountain (556 m), a walk that should definitely include a trip on the Kipphorn. From there, a gorgeous view is to be had.

◀ LILIENSTEIN. The Lilienstein (lilly's stone, 415 m) is the most distinctive mesa in Saxon Switzerland and offers an excellent view. It is the only mesa to the right of the Elbe river and it lies inside the Elbe loop. The hike takes about three hours and is also a great experience in winter. On the plateau, a restaurant welcomes the wanderer, an inn that has existed on this spot since 1873. Already in 1708, August the Strong commissioned the building of a stair path on the southern flank.

▼ SULPHUR LICHEN. In general, lichen do not get much attention, even though there are thousands of species alone in Europe, and many more worldwide. They exist in the most manifold shapes and colors. Especially striking and easy to find are the yellow Sulphur Lichen, which are very common in Saxon Switzerland.

◄◄ THE "ZIRKELSTEIN" (left page, to be seen in the right of the picture). With its 384 meters, it is the smallest mesa in Saxon Switzerland. On its summit sits an about 40 m high sandstone rock. In its immediate proximity (picture to the right), there is the almost 350 m high "Kaiserkrone" (emperor's crown), the jagged remainder of a former mesa. Three individual rocks from a distance look like the corners of a crown, hence the name. The cliffs are an ideal area for rock climbers.

◄◄ BIZARRE ROCK FORMATIONS. These rock formations (picture left and top right), typical for Saxon Switzerland, are the result of erosion, of weathering processes for which the basis was created about 145 million years ago in the Cretaceous period. Back then, an ocean for millions of years deposited sand, which, under high pressure, was condensed to firm sandstone and, at the same time, drained. Sandstone is a sedimentary rock that is generated through the erosion, the transport and, subsequently, the deposit of sand grains consisting of quartz. In the top right picture, the climbing area Hirschgrund on the 14 km-long Caspar-David-Friedrich-Path, which leads along the Elbe river until Reinhardtsdorf/Schöna, can be seen.

◄ VIEW OF THE ZSCHIRNSTEINE. To be seen in the background is the "Großer Zschirnstein", with its 563 m, the highest elevation in the German part of Saxon Switzerland. This typical mesa consists of sandstone. It features two rock climbing summits, the big and the small Zschirnsteinturm.

◄ "KUHSTALL" – COWSHED, that is how the largest cave in the area of the sandstone rocks "Neuer Wildenstein" is called. And indeed, to the citizens of Lichtenhain, it served as a hiding place for their cattle in the Thirty Years' War, hence the name. The rock tunnel is 24 m long, 11 m high and 17 m wide – so it is quite a spacious "stable".

◄◄ CLIMBING ROCK IN BIELA VALLEY. The Elbe Sandstone Mountains are a paradise for rock climbers, as can easily be seen in the picture left. However, climbing here follows other rules than in other climbing areas like the Alps or other Central German Uplands. The reason for that is the sandstone. When it is wet, it becomes porous and decreases in strength. Therefore, climbing on wet rocks, for example in the rain, but also the use of metal securing means are prohibited. Nevertheless, there are countless routes for climbers to let off steam.

A very popular area for climbing, but also hiking, stretches out to the left of the Elbe river in Biela valley (340 to 486 m). The valley can be reached from Pirna on a mountain road leading through a scenic landscape and offering gorgeous views. Time and again, charming viewpoints invite one to stay.

Of a very distinctive character is the upper Biela valley. Numerous rock towers present themselves rising right out of the forest, which makes them an Eldorado for rock climbers, but also a fascinating sight for hikers.

▼ WEHLNADEL, so the name of this distinctive climbing rock, which poses somewhat greater demands to the sports climbers. The rock is situated in the vicinity of the Bastei near Rathen. Generally, wall climbing in the sandstone rocks of Saxon Switzerland is of rather lower degrees of difficulty. Who-ever is looking for quiet and peace in this region during high season, the holidays or on weekends, is unfortunately going to be disappointed. Often busloads of visitors pour into the attractive area. However, whoever has seen the landscape for himself understands its strong appeal, and can not actually hold a grudge against the many tourists...

In the immediate vicinity of the Bastei rock, one comes across the remnants of the former fortification Neurathen Castle. The town of Rathen itself, incidentally, is easily reached by train. The car is better left outside town, for only residents or hotel guests with a guest pass are allowed to park in town.

◄◄ **Barbarine at Pfaffenstein mountain** (in the picture left). One of the most interesting of the Saxon Switzerland mountains is the Pfaffenstein (434 m). On its southern side stands the Barbarine, a slim, almost 43 m high rock needle, which was climbed for the first time in 1905. The needle is considered the emblem of Pfaffenstein mountain. For rock climbing, however, it has been closed for a couple of years. Despite attempts to "renovate" it, climbing here seems to be too dangerous. Pfaffenstein itself offers numerous climbing areas, however, so that enthusiasts get their money's worth.

▲ **Kirnitzsch valley.** Near Bad Schandau, the little creek Kirnitzsch flows into the Elbe river, hence the name of the valley (picture above). The hiking path leads through a wild and romantic landscape, the valley is considered one of the most beautiful ones of the Elbe Sandstone Mountains. One of the attractions here certainly is the historical Kirnitzschtalbahn (Kirnitzsch valley railway), which has transported passengers on an eight kilometer track through the valley since 1898. Final stop is the Lichtenhain waterfall.

◄ **Pfaffenstein and Lilienstein** mountains in the evening sun. A picture as if from an idyllic post card. The blood red sun bids farewell to the day.

▼ **Herkulessäulen – "Pillars of Hercules"** in Biela valley. The Biela is a tributary stream of the Elbe river. Under the name of Hammerbach it springs from Bohemian Switzerland, the Czech part of the Elbe Sandstone Mountains, only to reach Saxon after a few kilometers, where it joins the "Dürre Biela" river. Near Königstein the creek flows into the Elbe river. With regard to climbing, the Biela valley with its 239 peaks is the biggest section of the Elbe Standstone Mountains, which are rich in climbing opportunities anyway.

Product Management: Dr. Reinhard Pietsch, Susanne Caesar
Typography & Layout: Dr. Alex Klubertanz, Munich
Editing: Dr. Alex Klubertanz, Munich
Translation: Denis Fodor, Munich
Text: Ulrike Bässler, Munich
Repros: Scanner Service, Verona
Cover Design: Anna Katavic, and use of a photograph of the Huber Picture Agency
Cartography: Astrid Fischer-Leitl, Munich
Production: Bettina Schippel, Christine Herzer
Printed in Slovenia by MKT Print, Ljubljana

All facts contained were carefully researched by the author in consideration of the latest information available and fact-checked by the publisher. However, legal responsibility may not be inferred. We are always grateful for advice and suggestions. The address for these is:

Bruckmann Verlag
Postfach 80 02 40
D–81602 München
E-Mail: lektorat@bruckmann.de

Front Cover: The Frauenkirche
Back Cover: The Zwinger, the Fürstenzug, old Masters, Cigar Manufatory "Yenidze"
Pages 6–7, 92–93: Panorama

All cover illustrations, as well those in the text, are by Bildagentur Huber, Garmisch-Partenkirchen.

BILDAGENTUR
HUBER

ISBN 978-3-7654-4609-2